Julie Tsang

Julie Tsang is an award-winning playwright from Glasgow. Her short play *Lilyburgh Lane* won the Scotland Short Play Award in 2017, and her play *The Family Unit* was longlisted for The Bruntwood Prize 2019.

Theatre credits include: *The Family Unit* (Barons Court Theatre), *Lilyburgh Lane* (Cumbernauld Theatre), *Home* (Wee Theatre Festival), *Troon* (Theatre 503), *The Sorry Story of the Angel and the Bear* (Tron Theatre).

Fix is Julie's debut production, produced by Unbroken Theatre in association with the Pleasance and Yellow Earth Theatre. It was developed as part of Yellow Earth Theatre's Professional Writers Programme 2017-2019 supported by the Esmée Fairbairn Foundation.

First published in the UK in 2020 by Aurora Metro Publications Ltd.
67 Grove Avenue, Twickenham, TW1 4HX 02032610000
www.aurorametro.com   info@aurorametro.com
Twitter @aurorametro
Facebook www.facebook.com/AuroraMetroBooks

Fix copyright © 2020 Julie Tsang

Cover image courtesy of Rachel Wingate

All rights are strictly reserved.

For rights enquiries including performing rights, please contact the publisher: rights@aurorametro.com

No part of this publication may be reproduced, stored in or introduced into a retrieval system, or transmitted in any form, or by any means (electronic, mechanical, photocopying, recording or otherwise) without the prior permission of the publisher. Any person who does any unauthorised act in relation to this publication may be liable to criminal prosecution and civil claims for damages.

This paperback is sold subject to the condition that it shall not, by way of trade or otherwise, be lent, resold, hired out, or otherwise circulated without the publisher's prior consent in any form of binding or cover other than that in which it is published and without a similar condition being imposed on the subsequent purchaser.

Printed in the UK by 4edge Limited
ISBNs: 978-1-912430-49-9 (print)
978-1-912430-50-5 (ebook)

Unbroken Theatre in association with
the Pleasance and Yellow Earth Theatre
presents

Fix

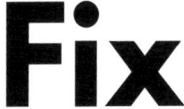

by
Julie Tsang

AURORA METRO BOOKS

for my Dad

CONTENTS

CAST & CREATIVES 6

BIOGRAPHIES 7

ABOUT THE THEATRE 12

ABOUT THE COMPANY 14

FIX 15

CAST

Li Na	Tina Chiang
Kevin	Mikey Anthony-Howe

CREATIVE TEAM

Writer	Julie Tsang
Director	Jen Tan
Designer	Rachel Wingate
Lighting Designer	Ali Hunter
Sound Designer	Richard Bell
Assistant Director	Zhui Ning Chang
Production and Stage Manager	Zoe Smith
Producer	Lian Wilkinson for Unbroken Theatre
Press Representation	Kate Morley PR

With thanks to: Caroline Jester, Kumiko Mendl, Tammie Rhee, Chris Corner, Stephen Hoo, Siu-See Hung, Julia Sandiford, David Lee Jones, Kelsey Yuhara, Masaaki Sagara, Mirai Nakamura, Alastair Gibbs at Apex Appliance Experts, Rosie Sharville, Playwrights' Studio Scotland, Adrian Hon, Six to Start, Ellie Simpson and Nic Connaughton.

Fix had a rehearsed reading at Soho Theatre on 22 March 2019 as part of the Yellow Earth Professional Writers Programme. This production of *Fix* has been supported by Arts Council England, the Cockayne Foundation and Greenwich Theatre.

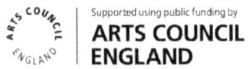 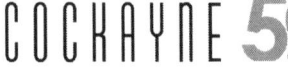 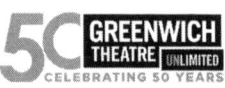

Biographies

CAST

Tina Chiang (Li Na)

Tina studied at RADA.

Theatre credits include: *E8* (Pleasance/The North Wall), *Mountains: The Dreams of Lily Kwok* (Royal Exchange Theatre/Yellow Earth Theatre), *Labour of Love* (Noel Coward Theatre), *Chimerica* (Harold Pinter Theatre), *Cyrano de Bergerac* (Southwark Playhouse), *Fox Attack* (National Theatre of Scotland/Oram Mor), *M. Butterfly* (GBS, RADA), *Why the Lion Danced* (UK Tour, Yellow Earth Theatre).

TV credits include: *Bodyguard, Silent Witness, Good Omens, Chimerica, Rellik, Kiss Me First, Fearless, Coronation Street, Emmerdale, Casualty, Run.*

Radio includes: *The Birthday Gift, The Last of the Pearl Fishers, Inspector Chen Mysteries.*

Mikey Anthony-Howe (Kevin)

Mikey Anthony-Howe graduated from Arts Educational in 2017 and is an alumnus of Yellow Earth Academy.

Mikey made his professional theatre debut as Lee in *Privates on Parade* (Union Theatre).

Further credits include: Demetrius/Francis Flute/Mustardseed in *A Midsummer's Night Dream* (Applecart Theatre), Carl in the web series *That's My Chair,* and appearances in a number of short films including *Back Row* and *Bruiser Boy.*

CREATIVE TEAM

Jen Tan (Director)

Jen Tan is a director and actor. She trained at The Oxford School of Drama and on the StoneCrabs Young Directors' Programme. Her work spans theatre, film, gaming and audio.

Theatre credits include: *A.I.D.A.N* by Matilda Ibini and *Of Being Alone in a Forest* by Tom Morton-Smith (Miniaturists), *Romeo & Juliet* (Papergang Theatre), *Being Norwegian* by David Greig (StoneCrabs/Albany Theatre) and as Assistant Director on *Tao of Glass* (Manchester International Festival). She also co-created verbatim play, *I Walk in Your Words*, with Kristine Landon-Smith for Tamasha.

Rachel Wingate (Designer)

Rachel Wingate is the Associate Designer to Soutra Gilmour.

Theatre credits include: *Manuelita* (Popelei Theatre, UK and South American Tour), *Burnt Part Boys* (Park Theatre), *Earthquakes in London* and MA Triple Bill (Arts Ed), *Islands* (Edinburgh Festival and Pleasance) and *In Doggerland* (Box of Tricks, National Tour).

As Associate Designer: *& Juliet* (Manchester Opera House and Shaftesbury Theatre), *Betrayal* (Harold Pinter Theatre and Bernard B. Jacobs Theater), *Pinter at the Pinter Season* (Harold Pinter Theatre), *Quartett* (Opera de Rouen Normandie), *Reasons to be Happy* (Hampstead); *The Ruling Class* (Trafalgar Studios) and *Bull* (Young Vic).

Ali Hunter (Lighting Designer)

Theatre credits include: *L.O.V.E* (Arielle Smith's Project DOT), *The Man who wanted to be a Penguin* (Stuff and Nonsense); *Mother of Him* (Park Theatre), *For Services Rendered, The Play About my Dad, Woman before a Glass* (Jermyn Street), *Cash Cow* (Hampstead), *Muckers* (The Egg, Conde Duque, Oxford Playhouse), *Soft Animals* (Soho), *Sugar, Don't Forget the Birds, Rattlesnake* (Open Clasp), *I know not these my hands, Happy Fathers' Day, Sugarman* and *All in Minor* (The Place), *Clear White Light* (Live Theatre Newcastle), *Treemonisha, The Boatswain's Mate* (Arcola), *Fairytale Revolution, Out of Sorts, Isaac Came Home from the Mountain, Cinderella and the Beanstalk* (Theatre 503).

As Associate Lighting Designer: *Hot Mess for Candoco Dance, The Half God of Rainfall* (Birmingham Rep and Kiln) Lighting Designer: Jackie Shemesh.

Ali is the Young Associate Lighting Designer for Matthew Bourne's *Romeo and Juliet.* Lighting Designer: Paule Constable.

Richard Bell (Sound Designer)

Richard has been working in technical theatre for over twelve years, in recent years focusing on sound design.

Theatre credits include: *Dead Equal* and *A Table Tennis Play* (both Edinburgh Fringe), *The Ladykillers, Beauty and the Beast, Single Spies* (all Theatre by the Lake), *The Game of Love and Chai* (Tara Arts and UK Tour) and *The End of Hope* (Soho Theatre/Orange Tree Theatre).

Credits as Associate Sound Designer: *The Funeral Director* (UK Tour), *Caroline's Kitchen* (UK Tour), *The Astonishing Vacuum Cleaner* (Dukes Lancaster and UK Tour), *Hogarth's Progress* (Rose Theatre Kingston) and

Misty (Trafalgar Studios). Richard has also worked on the hugely successful iPhone/android running app, *Zombies, Run!*

Zhui Ning Chang (Assistant Director)

Zhui Ning Chang is a Malaysian theatre director and producer based in London. Her practice focuses on intercultural performance, multilingual theatre, and new writing from underrepresented communities. Zhui Ning is an Associate Director at Flux Theatre and Connections Producer at Global Voices Theatre. Venues and companies she worked with include the Roundhouse, Rich Mix, Tamasha Theatre, Park Theatre, and VAULT Festival.

Past directing credits include: *Tamasha Scratch Night* (Soho Theatre), *Tango* (Yellow Earth Theatre), *Inside Voices* (VAULT 2019, Origins Award for Outstanding New Work).

Zoe Smith (Production and Stage Manager)

Zoe Smith has worked across a variety disciplines of technical theatre, including stage management, lighting, sound and video. She is currently a technician at the Theatre Royal Concert Hall in Nottingham and volunteers at the Nottingham New Theatre as External Relations Manager.

Stage Management credits include: *When I Watch You, I Like to Leave the Sound Off, Twelfth Night, Breathing Holes, The Beauty Queen of Leenane, NSFW* and *Cogito Ergo Bum* (all Nottingham New Theatre). Zoe has also worked as a technician at the National Student Drama Festival.

Lian Wilkinson (Producer)

Lian Wilkinson is a theatre producer, having most recently worked as the Sustained Theatre Regional Associate Producer at Belgrade Theatre Coventry before joining Yellow Earth as Executive Producer.

Lian has also worked for English Touring Theatre and in the technical and production department of the COMEDIA Theater in Cologne, Germany.

Credits include: *Under the Umbrella* (Belgrade Theatre and UK Tour), *Meet Me in the Ruins, Building Bridges* (both Belgrade Theatre), *We Live by the Sea* (Adelaide Fringe and 59E59 Theaters), and *Honk!* (Union Theatre).

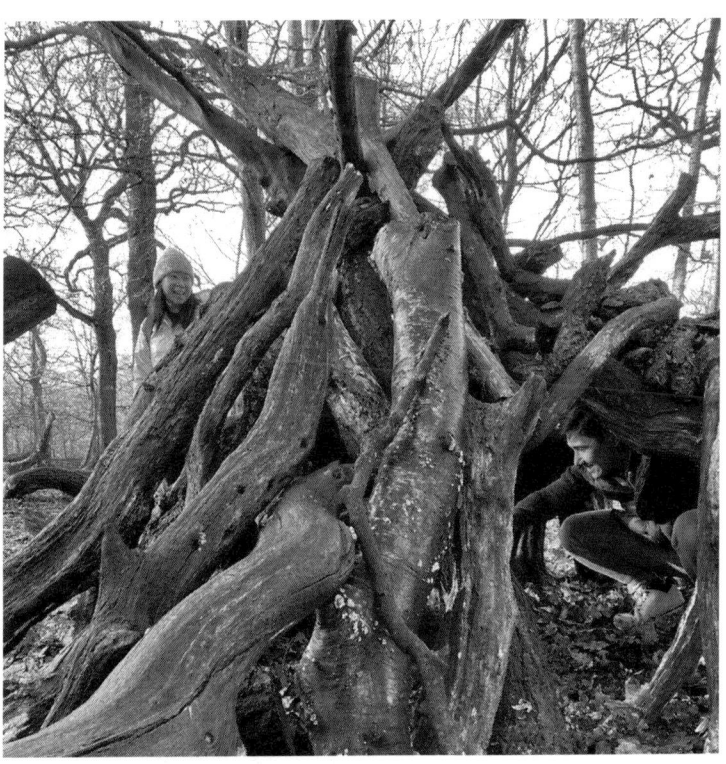

PLEASANCE THEATRE TRUST

Pleasance Edinburgh opened as part of the 1985 Festival Fringe with two theatres facing onto a deserted courtyard-come-car-park at an unfashionable eastern end of Edinburgh's Old Town. Thirty seasons later the Pleasance has become one of the biggest and most highly respected venues at the Edinburgh Festival Fringe, with an international profile and a network of alumni that reads like a Who's Who of contemporary comedy, drama and entertainment.

Pleasance Islington has been one of the most exciting Off-West-End theatres in London since it opened its doors in 1995, providing a launch pad for some of the most memorable productions and renowned practitioners of the past decade and staying true to its mission of providing a platform for the talent of the future. Across three-spaces, the theatre welcomes artists at all stages of their careers, with a commitment to new work that pushes boundaries.

Pleasance Islington plays host to some of the biggest names in comedy and the likes of Michael McIntyre, Russell Brand, Micky Flanagan, Mark Watson, Adam Hills and Mark Thomas have all regularly complimented our comedy programme.

For the Pleasance:

Anthony Alderson	Hamish Morrow
DIRECTOR	GENERAL MANAGER
Nic Connaughton	Ryan Taylor
HEAD OF THEATRE	HEAD OF COMEDY

Yvonne Goddard
HEAD OF FINANCE

Jonny Patton
ASSOC. PROGRAMMER

Stuart Hurford
MARKETING MANAGER

Robbie Porter
GRAPHIC DESIGNER

Emily Holland
BOX OFFICE DEPUTY MANAGER

Ryan Ford
VENUE TECHNICIAN

Eppie Conrad
VENUE TECHNICIAN

Jared Hardy
FINANCE ASSISTANT

Ellie Simpson
PRODUCER

Conor O'Donnelly
MARKETING OFFICER

Kathleen Price
BOX OFFICE MANAGER

Thomas Wortley
VENUE TECHNICIAN (INTERIM)

Marec Joyce
TECHNICAL DIRECTOR

Dan Smiles
THEATRE MANAGER

·PLEASANCE·

YELLOW EARTH THEATRE

Yellow Earth creates, nurtures and champions the best of British East Asian (BEA) Theatre. We seek out East Asian artistic talent and provide high quality creative opportunities for BEA theatre practitioners to develop work that is bold in both form and content and challenges the status quo. We bring unheard voices and stories to audiences from all backgrounds through touring productions, site-specific work and public readings. We also provide professional development programmes for writers and actors, and outreach work in schools and museums.

2020 marks Yellow Earth's 25th anniversary.

Find out more at: www.yellowearth.org

@yellowearthuk

For Yellow Earth:
ARTISTIC DIRECTOR
Kumiko Mendl
EXECUTIVE PRODUCER
Lian Wilkinson
ASSOCIATE PRODUCER
Tammie Rhee

BOARD OF TRUSTEES:
Wai Mun Yoon (Chair), Katie Elston, Maninder Gill, Richard Shannon, Kithmini Wimalasekera

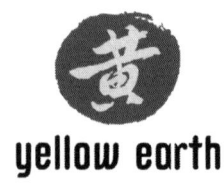

FIX

Julie Tsang

The first performance of *Fix* was at the Pleasance Theatre in Islington on 14 January, 2020.

CHARACTERS
LI NA – Female
KEVIN – Male

LOCATION
Tree and House

1. TREE

LI NA   Once. A long, long time ago,
There was a tree.
A momentous tree.
A magnificent tree towering over us in the middle of the woods.
It stood on six legs that splayed out and moved down, burying deep underground.

2. HOUSE

Kevin begins speaking off-stage during the speech then enters the room followed by Li Na. He rubs his temples.

KEVIN It was a nightmare trying to find this place. You're right off the grid.
Google maps had me all over the place.
Round and round I went, in circles. No signal. Nothing but tree after tree after tree. Almost turned back...

LI NA Why didn't you?

KEVIN Dunno. Curiosity. A job's a job you know? Times like these, can't be knocking back the work now, can I?

LI NA Shall we begin?

KEVIN Eh? Oh, yea right. So, what's the problem then?

LI NA There was an awful bang. A clanging metal sound. A huge noise filling the room.

KEVIN Sounds like the drum.

LI NA Does that normally...?

KEVIN It happens.

LI NA Ah...

KEVIN Is it switching on?

LI NA Yes, it lights up perfectly. Like Blackpool illuminations.

KEVIN Ha, yea. Is there a light in this room?

LI NA Once there is power in the machine there is no need for light.

KEVIN Can't it be switched on if I'm to fix it?

LI NA Of course.

Li Na switches on the light. A small bulb hangs precariously from the ceiling giving a dim pool of light. Kevin moves towards the machine, it has been moved forward out from the wall, he moves it out to give him more space around the back.

KEVIN Did you move this yourself? It's a ton weight!

Kevin looks at Li Na, seeing her better in a lit room, he turns his attention to the machine, inspecting the back with a small torch. He pulls a screwdriver from his pocket. He starts to dismantle the back. His head disappears behind the machine. Li Na observing this stranger in her home. Sounds of clanging metal.

LI NA So, what's your story?

KEVIN My story?

LI NA Did you have far to travel? *(Raises voice)* Did you have far to travel?

KEVIN Eh? No, not really, I was in the area, well just on the edge of the woods.

LI NA That was fortunate.

KEVIN What?

LI NA I said that was convenient.

KEVIN Until I got lost. This house wasn't easy to find, you know, all those trees out there.

LI NA It is easy when you know your way.

KEVIN I didn't think there were any houses out this far. I don't remember ever seeing any.

LI NA You've been here before?

KEVIN Every kid has been in these woods. Nothing else to do around here. Well, there wasn't for me when I was a boy. Do they still come down here? Kids? Teenagers? *(Li Na shakes her head)* Ah, times have changed. It's funny, I just don't remember this place. A house out here in the middle of the woods. And I knew this place like the back of my hand!

LI NA This house has been standing here for a long, long time.

KEVIN I can tell.

LI NA Maybe you didn't know this place as well as you thought you did.

KEVIN Huh. It was a while ago.

LI NA And the trees keep growing, expanding, taking a new shape each year. I'm not surprised you don't remember it. Things look different to us as children. Our perspective changes as we grow.

KEVIN Yea that makes sense. It's quite strange being back here.

LI NA Strange?

KEVIN Yea, you know... nostalgic or I dunno... something like that. We'd play up the river. Skipping school. What a laugh we'd have, cutting about, climbing trees, building dens and dams, pulling all-nighters, telling stories around a fire! Those were the days... Ha. And now I'm right back where I started!

LI NA You moved away?

KEVIN Yea, we did. Far from here... When I

was about... dunno, young, I was young... *(Scratches his head in thought)*

LI NA *(change)* Am I your last call?

KEVIN What?

LI NA Am I your last call for today?

KEVIN Yea, yea, you're my last for today.

He glances at his phone, checking time, gets back to the machine. Tinkers with the back, wiping his hands on his trousers. Li Na watches him.

KEVIN Right, well, it's lost its bearings

LI NA Lost its bearings?

KEVIN They've worn away and now it's all out of alignment.

LI NA ...

KEVIN You know, off kilter. It's damaged the drum. *(Shakes head)* Big job. You'd be better off buying a new one.

LI NA *(disbelief)* A new machine?

KEVIN For the price of new parts, the drum, labour, you're talking...

LI NA I don't want a new machine.

KEVIN It's going to be expensive.

LI NA I like this one.

KEVIN You'd be better off –

LI NA I have money.

KEVIN Look Mrs...

LI NA Li Na.

KEVIN Eh?

LI NA My name is Li Na.

KEVIN OK, Li Na. Look, you can order a new one online and they'll deliver it in a couple of days. If they can find this place that is...

LI NA There's no internet here.

KEVIN Really?

LI NA You said yourself. No signal.

KEVIN Right, well... *(Thinks, checks phone)* OK, so it's only four. If you head now, the shops might still be open...

LI NA I don't want a new one.

KEVIN There are lots of newer models.

LI NA I like this one.

Kevin keeps trying to get online.

KEVIN Ah, shit. Look I'm only trying to save you money.

LI NA Money is for spending.

KEVIN Then spend it on a new machine. No brainer! Look, you're talking a hundred and fifty to two hundred quid just for parts.

LI NA That's fine.

KEVIN You'd be as well flushing your money down the toilet. And there's no guarantee it'll work! *(Li Na is obviously distressed)* I'm only trying to help you.

LI NA I have the money. In cash. Upstairs.

KEVIN Look, I'm not the type of person to rip

you off, OK? There's enough of them out there, believe me.

LI NA Then what type of person are you?

KEVIN *(taken aback)* I'm just being honest with you. Have a think about it. It's a lot of money to waste…

LI NA I need it working tonight. I need you to fix it now.

KEVIN I don't think I have the right parts with me.

LI NA I need it. I need to use it.

KEVIN Why don't you think it over tonight, and if you still want it fixed, I'll come back tomorrow?

LI NA You'll come back?

KEVIN Yea.

LI NA You won't come back. You can fix it tonight.

KEVIN Mrs… Li Na, look…

LI NA Do you have a family?

KEVIN Eh?

LI NA A wife? I don't see a ring. A girlfriend? A boyfriend? A lover of any sort?

KEVIN What has that go to do with it?

LI NA If the answer is 'no' then why rush home? I know you want to get back after working all day but if there is no one waiting…

KEVIN I have a cat to feed.

Li Na takes bank notes from her apron, she holds them out for Kevin.

KEVIN   That's a lot of money.

LI NA   I don't go outside so I can't buy a new one. Please? *(Beat, a moment.)* They look at each other.

Still for a moment.

KEVIN   You don't go outside? You don't leave this house? *(Li Na shakes her head. Kevin thinks, takes the money.)* OK. OK, maybe I could... I'll see what I can do.

Li Na is relieved. Kevin tries to make light of the situation.

KEVIN   You really want it fixed, eh?

He busies himself with the machine, looks through his toolbox, takes out metal parts, nuts, bolts and stuffs them in his pockets.

LI NA   Do you think you have the right parts?

KEVIN   Eh? Yea, yea, I think I can use these to balance the weight out... *(Beat)* Look, the bearings have practically worn away. If I fix this up now it could go on the blink again tomorrow!

LI NA   I'm prepared for that.

KEVIN   You can't keep mending it; it's old, eventually it'll pack in and once it's done, it's done

LI NA   He who sups with the devil should have a long spoon.

KEVIN   You what?

LI NA   It means when taking a risk, one has to live with the consequences of their actions.

KEVIN   Right... *(confused)*

LI NA   It's a proverb.

KEVIN Yea? I never paid any attention in school.

LI NA I am prepared for whatever the outcome may be.

Kevin prepares to mend the machine, doing a sort of handyman ritual, stretches arms out, stares at the machine, sizing up his opponent.

KEVIN I'm going to need more light in here. *(He switches the torch on but it isn't enough.)*

LI NA I can hold it for you.

KEVIN You're alright. *(He steadies the torch on the machine.)* Do you think you could open the curtains, let some light in?

LI NA I'm afraid I can't do that.

KEVIN It's really dark in here, Li Na, if I am to fix this machine –

LI NA They are for show.

KEVIN For show?

LI NA They don't budge. Not very practical for situations like this. Sorry.

KEVIN You really do like wasting your money, eh?

LI NA I'm starting to regret purchasing them now.

KEVIN So am I.

Li Na watches Kevin closely, he feels her eyes on him.

KEVIN This is buying into my beer time, you know.

LI NA I have beer.

KEVIN Got the van outside.

LI NA Of course. *(She examines the toolbox.)* I've always wondered why there are so many different screwdriver heads. Wouldn't life be simpler with just one size that fits all! Then there wouldn't be the need to carry all these bits and pieces around.

Kevin pops his head up, sees Li Na holding a screwdriver.

KEVIN That's the one.

She hands it to him. He turns his attention back to the machine. Li Na takes another tool from the box; it's not a screwdriver, looks more like a metal rod, sharp and knife like. She studies it, then carefully places it in her apron, her eyes on Kevin.

LI NA Do you really have a cat?

KEVIN You what?

LI NA Do you have a cat?

KEVIN I don't make a habit of lying about pets.

LI NA You don't look like a cat person.

KEVIN No? *(He looks up at Li Na)* You don't look like a beer drinker.

Li Na laughs. Kevin turns back to the machine.

LI NA What colour is your cat?

KEVIN Black and brown and orange... and bits of white. She's got white specks around her nose.

LI NA She?

KEVIN Suzi.

LI NA Suzi.

KEVIN Yep. That's my girl.

LI NA I like it when animals have proper names. It humanises them.

KEVIN Yea, well she's a bloody bitch at times. Scratches all the furniture, climbs over my head when I'm trying to sleep, hides my keys...

LI NA Your keys?

KEVIN Oh yea, she's wild. Look at my arms. *(He lifts sleeves to reveals scratches.)* It was completely uncalled for.

LI NA An unprovoked attack.

KEVIN Yea, yea exactly!

LI NA They do that when they are young?

KEVIN I've had her for more than ten years! You know what, I think she's secretly plotting to kill me.

Li Na laughs, louder than the last time. Kevin feels uneasy with Li Na's response, he laughs a little.

LI NA Do you have a photo of Suzi?

KEVIN Eh no, why would I? She's not a baby.

LI NA You might want to look at her sometimes.

Kevin gets up, goes for another tool.

KEVIN I see her every night.

LI NA I like to keep photos. I think it's a nice thing to do. So you always have it. An image to store. Like a memory, so you get every little detail right and don't forget...

KEVIN I'll not forget what she looks like in a hurry. I am constantly reminded of her presence! *(Refers to the scratches on his arms.)*

LI NA Ha.

KEVIN It's the way it is now, people taking photos and sticking them up all over Facebook, Instagram - Cats of Instagram and all that nonsense.

LI NA Poisons your brain.

KEVIN You are dead right!

LI NA I have lived without the need for modern technology all of my life and it has served me well.

KEVIN Yea? Good for you! So wait, what about a mobile phone?

LI NA Nope.

KEVIN No mobile? Really? You know I have thought about it myself. But well, I can't give it up, not with my line of work, imagine me having to rely on the old landline!

LI NA No home telephone either.

KEVIN You what? Fair enough without a mobile, but to be out here in the middle of the woods with no phone? I've got to hand it to you. If you had to meet someone you just set a date, showed up on time, you know. None of this texting because you're running late... *(has a realisation)* Wait, hold on, how did you call me?

LI NA That is a good question.

KEVIN ...?

LI NA There's a telephone box across the back of the forest, beyond the river. Don't you remember it?

KEVIN No, there isn't.

LI NA Yes, there is.

KEVIN No, there isn't it.

LI NA Yes, there is.

KEVIN I know these woods...

LI NA Like the back of your hand.

KEVIN No, I'd have remembered...

LI NA Didn't you say you moved away?

KEVIN Yea, but...

LI NA Then you have forgotten.

KEVIN No, wait, wait...I thought you didn't like going outside.

LI NA I do like going outside.

KEVIN Then why were you making a fuss about it earlier?

LI NA The telephone box is exactly four point five kilometres away, a brisk walk on a dry day will take you eighteen minutes to get there, twenty-five minutes on a wet day. It is a rare occurrence for me to go outside but in an emergency like this, well, it had to be done.

KEVIN So you're saying there's a telephone box twenty minutes away from this place?

LI NA Eighteen minutes on a dry day.

KEVIN Nah, I drove around here, there was

nothing for miles.

LI NA You were driving on the road?

KEVIN Yea, but...

LI NA Then how would you have seen it?

KEVIN But I know these woods...

LI NA You keep saying woods, like this is some kind of children's bedtime story. We are in a forest, Kevin.

KEVIN What's the difference?

LI NA Woods are smaller, significantly less dense. The trees around here grew up to the sky and down in the earth. Roots connected, entwined and multiplied. Resulting in a greater mass.
I have lived with these trees and watched them grow. You have been away from here for too long, you don't see it. Or you have simply forgotten...

KEVIN A telephone box?

LI NA Yes. A telephone box. *(Kevin is perplexed and not convinced.)* If you don't believe me, you can go out to see it for yourself.

KEVIN Nah, nah, I believe you it's just.... weird that there's a telephone box out in the middle of the woods, forest, that's all.

LI NA Well, it's come in very handy for me.

KEVIN I can imagine it has! *(Beat)* Right where was I? *(Pulls phone from his pocket to check time.)* Shit, right better get on with this... Ah this one might work.

Kevin looks at the tool box, he notices something missing.

LI NA How rude!

KEVIN You what?

LI NA You have been here all this time and I haven't offered you a refreshment! Would you like some tea?

KEVIN This shouldn't take much longer, if I could just find...

LI NA I could get you a coffee if you'd prefer something a little stronger.

KEVIN I was sure it was in here the last time I checked...

LI NA Or a glass of water?

KEVIN Nah, nah, you're alright... *(Scratches head, continues to look through tool box, looking at floor.)*

LI NA Have you lost something?

KEVIN I saw it earlier; I saw it in this box.

LI NA Let me help you.

KEVIN Nah, I don't need any help.

LI NA What is it you're looking for?

KEVIN I swear I had it in here...

LI NA I can check if I have something similar you could use.

KEVIN I don't need it for this job, it's just, it's not here anymore...

LI NA If you tell me what it is you have lost–

KEVIN I haven't lost it.

LI NA	OK.
KEVIN	It was here.
LI NA	If you tell me–
KEVIN	I saw it.
LI NA	Can you describe it? Maybe I can...
KEVIN	Did you take it?
LI NA	Take what?
KEVIN	One of my tools.
LI NA	What type of tool?

KEVIN   It's... it's... for... Did you move any of my things?

LI NA   Are you looking for this? *(She takes the tool from her pocket and holds it up pointing sharp end at his chest.)* I don't know how I ended up with it! *(She holds it out, like a knife, a weapon, slightly intimidating. Kevin puts his hand out to take it from her.)*

KEVIN   Can I have it back?

She holds it still for a moment longer.

LI NA   It's very sharp, I wonder what it's used for?

KEVIN   It's just a tool.

LI NA   I'd be extra careful with it. You don't want it getting into the wrong hands. I must have taken it for safe keeping.

KEVIN   I'll keep it out the way, safely. Can I have it back now? Please?

She turns the sharp end towards her to hand it over safely.

KEVIN Please don't touch my tools. They're expensive to replace. *(He puts the tool in his back pocket. Li Na gives a hands-up gesture, she goes to the kettle.)*

LI NA *(change in mood)* How do you take your tea?

KEVIN *(suspicious)* I'm okay for tea. *(He rubs his head.)*

LI NA Headache?

KEVIN Eh, yea actually.

LI NA I've boiled the kettle, a warm drink might ease the pain.

KEVIN It's okay.

LI NA It's not a problem. I insist.

KEVIN Alright then.

Li Na busies herself at the kettle, Kevin watches her, her back to him. His hand on the tool in his pocket.

KEVIN It's quite a place you've got here, have you lived here long?

LI NA All my life.

KEVIN And you live out here on your own?

LI NA I do. *(He moves towards her.)*

KEVIN Must be so quiet out here... I take it you don't get many visitors?

LI NA No, I don't.

KEVIN *(approaching Li Na)* Funny how I don't remember this place... Or you...

A noise is heard above them, upstairs. A banging, like something heavy has been knocked over. Kevin is startled by the sound.

KEVIN What was that? *(Li Na is unfazed by the sound.)* Did you hear that?

LI NA *(turns)* Huh?

Another thud is heard, not as loud as the first but audible.

KEVIN That? *(He moves to investigate. Li Na shakes her head.)*

LI NA Are you sure you heard something?

KEVIN It was deafening! *(She moves towards him. They listen.)* Is someone up there?

Another thudding sound, but quieter than the first.

KEVIN There!

LI NA Ah!

KEVIN You heard it?

LI NA I did.

KEVIN Well, what is it?

LI NA *(thinks)* I'm not entirely sure.

KEVIN Is someone up there? You said you lived here on your own!

LI NA I do. *(Thudding again)*

KEVIN I'm going up.

LI NA I wouldn't do that.

KEVIN Why not?

LI NA It's probably... my cat.

KEVIN Your cat?

LI NA   Black with white paws.

KEVIN   You didn't tell me you had a cat.

LI NA   You didn't ask me. Zhen Zhen... My cat...

KEVIN   It sounds more like an elephant.

LI NA   Oh you know how it is with them jumping off the furniture, knocking things over, hiding keys...

KEVIN   Does anyone else live here with you?

LI NA   Just Zhen Zhen and me.

Kevin looks up at the ceiling again not convinced.

KEVIN   Do you know you've got a huge crack on your ceiling?

LI NA   Uh huh. *(She nods, goes back to the tea, and the noise has stopped. Li Na isn't concerned with the crack.)*

KEVIN   Zhen Zhen?

LI NA   It means very precious. Zhen Zhen is very important to me. Just like your Suzi is to you, yes?

KEVIN   You should get that seen to. *(Pointing to the cracks on the ceiling)* Or Zhen Zhen will fall through one of these days!

LI NA *(laughs)*   One thing at a time.

Kevin keeps his eyes still on the ceiling, but there is no more noise. He moves back to the machine, has a look around the room.

KEVIN   So, where is your photo of this Zhen Zhen? Didn't you say if you had a cat you would keep a photograph, help you remember her or something?

Li Na points to a picture on the wall of a dragon.

KEVIN That's a dragon. A yellow dragon, not a cat.

LI NA It's a very good interpretation of her character. *(Kevin rubs his head.)*

LI NA Still in pain?

Kevin nods.

LI NA Here, drink this, it will help.

She hands Kevin a cup. Reluctantly at first, he drinks a little.

KEVIN So why do you need this machine fixed tonight? Off on a holiday?

LI NA No, nothing sinister like that.

KEVIN Sinister?

LI NA All that blistering heat, it's my idea of hell, actually. And all those beasties, I can barely cope with the disgusting creatures that lurk around here, seeping their way through the cracks in my walls. No thank you.

KEVIN You can go somewhere with a cooler climate you know.

LI NA And what would be the point in that?

KEVIN To get away.

LI NA I have no need to escape. Everything I need is under this roof. I am perfectly content here, well I was until my machine decided to stop functioning!

KEVIN Where is all your laundry then?

LI NA Do you normally ask all these questions when you respond to calls?

KEVIN I was just wondering what it is you need to wash so desperately that it can't wait till tomorrow, that's all.

LI NA He who asks questions is a fool for five minutes. He who does not ask questions at all, is a fool forever.

KEVIN Eh?

LI NA Drink up. It will help your headache.

Kevin looks into his cup. Drinks.

KEVIN It's a bit strong.

LI NA It will get rid of all those ghastly toxins.

KEVIN I don't think I need a detox.

LI NA Everyone must cleanse their body of sin.

KEVIN Sin? Has anyone ever told you, you have quite a way with words?

Kevin drinks it all. Shivers. Li Na takes the cup. Kevin looks out the window, something catches his eye, trees moving in the wind.

KEVIN Must get awful lonely out here, nothing but trees.

LI NA That's what everyone who lives in a city thinks. Just because you have people surrounding you, above you, below you, lights and noise, doesn't mean you can't get lonely.

KEVIN I suppose.

LI NA They say living in a city can be very isolating. *(Beat)* Why aren't you married?

KEVIN Sorry?

LI NA A handsome man like you, why aren't you taken?

KEVIN Well, I guess... I dunno... Maybe I haven't met the right...

LI NA Oh don't say that.

KEVIN What?

LI NA The right person. It's a ridiculous turn of phrase, don't you think?

KEVIN Is it?

LI NA Of course it is. If you believe there is a 'right' person out there just for you. The type of person who is never wrong because you set up this belief that they are right for you, they are the one, they can do no wrong. So when they eventually do wrong, like all people do... you feel betrayed. Hurt. Ashamed. But let's face it, we're only human. We all make mistakes, don't we?

KEVIN ...I guess...

LI NA Do you like being on your own?

KEVIN Dunno. Sometimes.

LI NA Then say that. Say you enjoy your life as a single man. Easy.

KEVIN Are you married?

LI NA In reality or fantasy?

KEVIN ...

LI NA Reality – no. Fantasy – yes.

KEVIN *(thinks)* Well that's nice, it can happen for you.

LI NA No, it can't.

KEVIN Of course it can, you just have to get out there, meet new people, you know?

LI NA Perhaps in another life. More tea?

KEVIN Nah, I'll be pissing all night, sorry.

LI NA I'm not offended.

KEVIN I'll get back to it. *(Goes to machine)*

LI NA Very well, Kai Wen.

KEVIN *(surprised)* What did you? I didn't tell you my name.

LI NA You did.

KEVIN I don't... that's not my name. I'm Kevin.

LI NA OK, Kevin.

KEVIN Why did you call me... I haven't used that ... *(Scratches head)* in a long time.... I'm Kevin, my name is... Kevin...

LI NA You came to my door and introduced yourself by name, then you told me about how you got lost and your Sat Nav...

KEVIN Google maps, I don't have a Sat Nav.

LI NA Google maps, said you were way off the grid...

KEVIN Yea, yea I did say that.

LI NA Nothing but tree after tree after tree.

KEVIN	Yea, yea...
LI NA	You played up by the river when you were a boy, skipping school, telling stories, building fires. You told me a lot about yourself, actually.
KEVIN	I did?
LI NA	And Suzi.
KEVIN	Suzi.
LI NA	Your cat.
KEVIN	Yea, yea, my cat.
LI NA	Are you feeling alright?
KEVIN	I'm just... my head...
LI NA	You're out of alignment.
KEVIN	Eh?
LI NA	Off kilter.
KEVIN	...
LI NA	Look, maybe this has been too much. Maybe you should rest for a moment.
KEVIN	No, I...
LI NA	You need to take a little time out.

The thudding sound is heard above them. Kevin is sensitive to the noise, holds his head.

KEVIN	What is that?

Li Na guides Kevin to a chair.

LI NA	Zhen Zhen! I'll kill her one of these days.
KEVIN	I never told you...

LI NA Come on Kevin.

Li Na helps Kevin into the chair, he is heavy, tired.

LI NA Just a few minutes.

KEVIN Wait... I...

LI NA That's all, just a few minutes to take your mind off the day...

KEVIN But I never told you my name...

Kevin sits on the chair, head lolling. Li Na watches him. The thudding is still resounding above them, quieter, a dull noise. With every thud, Kevin feels the pain in his head, he drifts off to sleep.

3. TREE

LI NA Once...
A long time ago in the woods, there was a tree,
A momentous tree.
A magnanimous tree.
With multiple arms stretching out extending to the sky
Crossing over to other trees, reaching, connecting, touching...

4. HOUSE

Interior room in the house, same as before. The machine, tools, everything remain untouched.

But the room is brighter. More light coming through the window. Shadows are created on the walls, it's an old house. Cracks run up the walls and across the ceiling. Old and tired feeling. Kevin rouses.

LI NA   Kevin, you've returned.

KEVIN   I was driving around and round. No signal. I couldn't get out... I couldn't...

LI NA   Bad dream?

KEVIN   Dream? No, I left and it was... *(He rubs his head.)*

LI NA   You got lost?

KEVIN   No, I know these woods... I knew these woods... Forest... I knew this forest...

LI NA   You didn't leave. Your tools are still here.

KEVIN   My tools.

LI NA   There, right where you left them.

Kevin stands, a little unsteady.

LI NA   Easy now, get your balance. *(She goes to help him, he moves away, takes out his phone.)*

KEVIN   Ah shit, it's not working.

LI NA   I told you there's no signal.

KEVIN   No, the time, it's, it's not the right... it says it's four, but when I got here it was ...what time is it?

Li Na looks to the shadows on the wall.

LI NA It is four o'clock

KEVIN Where is your clock?

LI NA I don't have one.

KEVIN So how do you know?

LI NA The shadows tell the time. I can work it out with how much sunlight I have on my wall. When the wall is completely black the sun has gone down.

KEVIN *(shaking phone)* What the hell? It's later than four, I've been here since... Look, I should go.

LI NA What about my machine?

KEVIN I'll come back another time.

LI NA You promised...

KEVIN I didn't promise nothing.

LI NA I gave you money. In cash. You said you would try to mend it...

KEVIN I tried and it didn't work.

LI NA You didn't try, all you've done is talk and then you had a sleep on my chair.

KEVIN You said I should rest... Look do you want the money back?

LI NA No, I want you to do what I paid you to do. I want you to fix my machine.

KEVIN And I told you it can't be fixed.

LI NA How would you know that when you haven't even tried? I wouldn't ask if I wasn't desperate.

KEVIN *(sighs)* Five minutes, I'll look at it for five minutes then I'm out of here.

LI NA Thank you. Shall we begin?

She gestures for him to take his place at the machine.

Kevin rubs his head, shivers, goes to the machine, starts to dismantle parts of the machine. Li Na watches him.

LI NA Perhaps you're sick.

KEVIN You what?

LI NA It seems like you are coming down with something. You should see a doctor.

KEVIN I'm fine... I'll have a look at this then I'll be on my way. Right, I just have to try and even this out...

Kevin holds his head, feeling out of balance himself. He feels less comfortable in the space, looks around the room, wary, confused. He looks at Li Na, notices the ceiling, the cracks are bigger, gaping, he stands up.

KEVIN Wow. That doesn't look good, you know. Is there a pipe up there? Water leaking?

LI NA No.

KEVIN That needs to be seen to.

LI NA I will.

KEVIN If you leave that any longer... I'm telling you, in this light that looks much worse. It could cave in. It's right down the walls. Jeez, what happened here?

LI NA It's an old house.

KEVIN There's water, look, look, there, it's leaking. I should take a look upstairs...

LI NA No need.

KEVIN It'll only take a minute.

LI NA This house is falling apart. It weeps. It needs love, it needs attention, it needs a lot of work. But right now what I need is for you to focus on fixing my machine.

He looks at the cracks above, little drops hanging ready to fall, uneasy with it. He sniffs, shivers, like he has the start of a cold. He looks at the drum, confused on where to start. Li Na now at the sink, takes clothing out from underneath.

KEVIN *(under his breath)* What do I know? Zhen Zhen not joining us?

LI NA Who?

KEVIN Your cat.

LI NA I don't have a cat.

KEVIN All the noise up there, you said it was your cat!

Li Na busies herself, she is either blatantly ignoring him or didn't hear.

LI NA Upstairs there is no cat. Upstairs there is a dragon.

KEVIN What? Oh, yea! The yellow dragon.

Li Na stops, watches him.

LI NA Do you know the story of the yellow dragon?

KEVIN Eh, no.

LI NA Your mother never read it to you as a child?

KEVIN No.

LI NA What about when you camped out here, you said you told stories to each other?

KEVIN Yea we did, but none about dragons. More like ghost stories, you know, spooky stuff to scare each other in the middle of the forest at night. *(He becomes uneasy at these thoughts.)*

LI NA Ah, the enchanted tree.

Kevin shakes his head.

LI NA You know, the monstrous tree that changes shape in the night. In the heart of this forest. The tree has a hollow base and there's an opening, you can climb inside and stand up.

KEVIN Yea, yea I think that rings a bell, actually.

LI NA You saw it?

KEVIN Yea, I think we did.

LI NA Who?

KEVIN My friends, we'd skip school and when it rained we climbed in for shelter, I'm sure we did... it was quite dark and scary... we would play hide and seek...

LI NA It was said that if you stayed in there for too long, the opening would close and you would be stuck inside for eternity...

KEVIN Yes, yes!... and your limbs would stretch and... and turn into roots!

LI NA You would become part of the tree.

KEVIN That's right! Ha, well, I'm glad I got

out of there! Is it still here? In this forest?

LI NA *(shrugs)* I don't go out often enough to check.

KEVIN It'll just be a big tree. Nothing else, just a story they made up around here to give us something to think about, saves us from boredom.

LI NA Stories give us a deeper connection and understanding for each other. Taking us away from the everyday to new exciting adventures.

KEVIN Yea, I always liked stories back then. They were like an escape, or something... *(beat)* So what's the deal with this yellow dragon then, it's a famous story or dragon or something?

LI NA Once...
A long, long time ago.
There was nothing
No nature. No creatures. No man. No woman.
Just a dark universe of chaos.
Disorder. Disarray.
But one day from the darkness emerged an egg
A simple sign of life
Of what could be
Inside the egg there were the perfectly opposed principles of Yin and Yang.
In time they balanced and shaped into the form of a primitive,
Horned and hairy giant named Pan Gu.
Pan Gu set out to create the world.
He a swung his giant axe and separating what was left of Yin from Yang.
Earth was created from Yin
The sky from Yang
To maintain this separation Pan Gu stood between the two and pushed them apart

Each day the sky grew ten feet higher
The earth ten feet wider
Pan Gu himself grew ten feet taller.
And after eighteen thousand years of creating the earth and sky, Pan Gu died.
His breath became the wind,
His voice the thunder,
His left eye the sun and his right eye the moon,
His hair turned into the brilliant night stars and the Milky Way.
His limbs became the mountains and other extremities that marked the four corners of the world.
From his muscles and sinew came the roots of the forest
His blood rivers
His teeth and nails metals and his bones rocks and minerals.
His bone marrow turned into sacred diamonds.
His sweat fell as rain.
For every essence of him became the world
His whole body split into the five elements, metal, wood, water, fire and earth...

KEVIN So hold on, this bolt here came from Pan Gu?

LI NA Everything in this world came from Pan Gu, so it was said.

KEVIN What about the dragon?

LI NA After Pan Gu's death there was a great flood and from the waters emerged the yellow dragon. A symbol of fertility. It laid three eggs: Heaven, Earth and Hell. We are all descendants of the dragon. We are reminded that this powerful beast came from our creator Pan Gu. From Man. Many people pray to the dragon 'Yinglong' in order to receive rain.

KEVIN   They must be praying hard around here.

LI NA   Hahaha yes. In this country there must be many believers!

Kevin lifts the drum to the machine.

KEVIN   Do you really believe all that?

LI NA   The question is, do you?

KEVIN   It seems a bit far-fetched, like Adam and Eve and all those myths.

LI NA   It happened or maybe it did not happen. The time is long past and much is forgotten, replaced, changed and fabricated into new versions of a story with more layers added to it each time it's told. What do you believe?

KEVIN   Science. Evolution. The big bang.

He whacks the drum with a hammer for effect, the noise creates an echo in the room. He starts to put it back into the machine.

LI NA   There are some things on this earth we don't understand but that doesn't mean they can't exist.

KEVIN   Don't. Don't exist.

Li Na is a little irked at his lack of openness.

LI NA   You are making a mess!

KEVIN   I just can't seem to get these parts back in, something's missing.

Li Na moves closer to inspect.

LI NA   You need something to fit in there to balance it.

KEVIN Yea, I'm aware of that

Li Na goes to the fireplace, she kicks a basket of woodblocks chips by accident, one piece falls out, Kevin sees it. He picks it up. He measures it against the drum – it fits!

LI NA Everything okay?

KEVIN Yea, yea I think this just might work... *(Surprisingly, it fits in to secure the drum)* I guess we can give it a go.

LI NA You know Kevin, in the earliest creation stories, it was actually a woman who created humans.

KEVIN Yea? *(Not really listening, his attention on the machine.)*

LI NA Her name was Nu Gua. She was an independent, powerful goddess. Bringing harmony to heaven, earth, and humanity. *(She moves to the other side of the machine, Kevin is on his knees working at the back, she watches him intently.)* But she became lonely. She walked plains and valleys and felt that the world was a desolate place. She wanted a new form of life, an extension of nature, so she sat beside the flowing waters and ran earth through her fingers,
Burying them deep, touching, connecting with the roots underground
Reaching, stretching, uniting with nature at its very core
From this she moulded water and earth into clay
Forming little creatures.
Little creatures with their own roots inside
A beating heart at their centre
Which brought them to life
They called her Mother and wandered the earth to

repopulate the world.

KEVIN Hold on, so if life started with this Nu Gua woman, why tell the Pan Gu story at all?

LI NA She was a self-aware, independent, creative, and powerful feminine force. Of course she was forgotten about. Her story changed,
Left out of all the books to be replaced by Pan Gu's
It's not the first time a woman's story is overthrown for a male version.
Would you have believed in the creation if it had all been started by a woman?

KEVIN Probably not. Regardless of who started it, man or woman, I would still feel the same.

LI NA Interesting...

KEVIN So why have the dragon, why don't you have a painting of Nu Gua or some other goddess?

LI NA Where?

KEVIN Up there, the yellow... Hey it's a snake.

LI NA A white serpent.

KEVIN No it was a dragon, I saw it, it was a yellow dragon!

LI NA Observation is very important in life, Kevin.

KEVIN No I remember. *(He shakes his head)* I could have sworn it was a dragon!

LI NA Sometimes we only see what we want to believe.

KEVIN It was a dragon. Wasn't it? *(Scratches*

his head) Maybe it was a snake...

Kevin feels confused so he tries to use the wood, busies himself.

Li Na goes to a small mirror sitting on the mantelpiece, she strokes her face, examining her lines. Noise from the machine.

KEVIN Hey! We have power, we have movement. Oh I think it's working! *(Stands back to admire his work, amazed it actually works.)* I fixed it! I actually fixed it!

LI NA How old do you think I am?

KEVIN Eh?

LI NA I'm starting to get lines. Embedding deep into my skin. Don't you think so? *(She turns to face Kevin.)*

KEVIN I wouldn't know...

LI NA Say whatever comes into your head, I will not be offended.

KEVIN Well, I haven't really looked at you properly.

LI NA Then look at me now.

KEVIN *(coy)* I'm really not so observant, as you pointed out with the dragon painting!

LI NA Snake.

KEVIN Yea, I mean snake! Eh, I guess you look younger than I first thought?

LI NA Really, what makes you say that?

KEVIN Eh, well, when I came here earlier, you looked...

And well now you look... And you live here on your own and well... It's a, it's an old house, with the décor and well it's just a bit...

LI NA What are you trying to say?

KEVIN Old?

LI NA I look 'old'

KEVIN No, not you. The house, the décor, it's old, but you're not... well, you're not that...

LI NA I'm not that what? Oh for goodness sake, spit it out!

KEVIN This house makes you look older than you probably are. I mean you are not as old as you, the house looks... and it's so dull in here! You look younger than you did earlier...which doesn't make any sense, maybe it's the light or lack of light in here...

He is worried he has offended Li Na, he turns and watches the machine's cycle slowly moving round. Pause.

LI NA I have done my best to make this a home!

KEVIN Look, what do I know? I don't have a lot to go by. Single man who lives with a cat! You just look younger than I first thought you were that's all, I was trying to give you a compliment

LI NA Do you usually judge someone at first impression?

KEVIN Doesn't everyone?

LI NA Not everyone.

KEVIN Hold on. You asked me how old I thought you looked.

LI NA Which you haven't replied to.

KEVIN You're the one making me judge you. And I hate answering that type of question. All I am saying is, you don't look old enough to be living in a place like this, that's all... this place ages you. It looks like it's dying!

LI NA It is dying. *(Beat)* So I should move to the city? Escape, run away far from here, like you did?

KEVIN I didn't run away, we moved.

LI NA Why?

KEVIN I didn't get a choice, I was a kid.

LI NA We all get a choice in what we do in life.

KEVIN No, no we don't. I didn't get to make that decision, it was made for me.

LI NA Do you always do what you're told?

KEVIN What? No.

LI NA You prefer to let someone else make the decision?

KEVIN Look, no, what are you getting at?

LI NA Someone else to take responsibility?

KEVIN You don't know anything about me! This is... what you're saying is way out of order. I'm doing you a favour here, I fixed your machine.

LI NA But you keep damaging it further. I don't think you can fix it Kai Wen.

KEVIN I can! I did!

The machine suddenly starts to grumble. The thudding from upstairs starts again, the machine jerks, loud noises fill the room.

LI NA You can't fix it.

Kevin goes to the machine, he holds it still; it shakes violently, it feels like the whole room and floor is shaking. Kevin is off kilter, the noise upstairs continues, together the sounds build, and then it all stops.

The machine is still, lights out and back panel falls off.

Kevin is defeated, looking drained, holding bits of the machine in his hands.

KEVIN You need a new machine! It's fucked! He picks up the pieces, the wood drops out. What was I thinking? Fucking wood!

LI NA Wood! You used the wood? Oh, Kevin. Ooooh, hahahah *(laughing)* You got carried away with Pan Gu's story! Men, ha! Metal, Water, Fire and Wood!

KEVIN You're the one that wants that piece of shit fixed, why don't you do it yourself? I'm out of here.

LI NA All things are difficult before they get easy!

KEVIN Stop laughing. *(He holds his head, the headache coming back.)*

LI NA Oh, I'm sorry.

KEVIN Stop it!

LI NA Tension is who you think you should be. Relaxation is who you are.

KEVIN Is that another fucking proverb?

LI NA I made it up. But it works for you, no?

Kevin pack his tools.

LI NA I shouldn't have interfered. It's my fault it didn't work. I'm not good around machinery. I am like a bad omen! *(She takes more money from her apron, she hands it out for him.)* You are right. I should give up. I should buy a new one.

KEVIN Then use the money to buy one.

LI NA No, please. It's for your work.

KEVIN I didn't fix it.

LI NA It's for your time.

Beat.

KEVIN I know it's none of my business and I don't know anything about you... But, it can't be good for you staying indoors all day. My van is outside. If you want, I can drop you in the city. There's a retail park you can go to have a look at new ones.

LI NA That's a kind gesture.

KEVIN *(shrugs)* Is there a reason why you can't go outside? *(She doesn't reply. He sighs)* Right well, I've got other calls to get to.

Kevin begins to pack his tools. Li Na moves back to the sink, she takes a bucket, she opens the washing machine door and takes out the sodden laundry, dampness fills the room, and Kevin begins to retch with the smell. Li Na goes to the kitchen cupboard under the sink, she brings out a small spray bottle and begins to spray the clothes, its scent fills the air.

KEVIN Oh, what is that? I know that smell. My mum used to use it on my clothes, I thought they stopped making it years ago! Sniffs the air. God, that takes me right back.

LI NA Back where?

Kevin in isolation.

KEVIN Our kitchen. Mum at the sink, the light coming through the window, sun shining in my eyes, blinding.
This silhouette of hers at the window.
She's telling me to stay. Don't move.
She's washing something in the sink.
The smell...
Flowers. Fresh.
The lights blinding.
Don't move.
She's saying something, I can't make it all out.
Something about my t-shirt...
Stains.
I must have been running through the mud, climbing the trees.
Don't move.
But it's not that.
She says it's not the mud.
It's definitely not mud.

Kevin is now back in Li Na's kitchen.

LI NA Are you okay?

KEVIN What...? I...

LI NA You were miles away. Sit down for a minute, Kevin. *(She helps him to a seat)* I'll get you some pain killers.

KEVIN No, no, I don't need them.

LI NA You are sick. This headache is

affecting you, you're all out of alignment, you need to take some medication.

KEVIN   I'm just tired...

LI NA   Have you eaten today?

KEVIN   I don't... I can't remember

LI NA   Just take a moment before you go.

Li Na gives Kevin some water, he gulps it down. She makes Kevin comfortable, a cushion at his back, he notices her neck, and a deep scar runs from her neck down her body. Kevin is taken aback.

KEVIN   Wow, what happened? *(She tries to cover it up. He notices her hands, they are scarred too)* Your hands? *(She quickly hides them away in her pocket.)*

KEVIN   What happened to you?

LI NA   An incident, a long time ago. I'll make you something to eat before you leave, just rest here a moment.

The light in the room slowly goes out, shadows cover the walls. Kevin's eyes grow heavy. The room descends into darkness.

5. TREE

LI NA   Once...
Some time ago
There stood a tree, a momentous tree,
a magnificent tree
With a beating heart in its centre.

If you listen, you can hear it beat and all the other sounds of its working body amplified within.

If you touch it you can feel its vibrations running throughout these entire woods.

6. HOUSE

From the window we can see it is dark outside. A crash of thunder is heard outside; a flash of lighting follows. It startles Kevin, who is eating a biscuit. The sound of him crunching is audible/heightened against the storm outside. Li Na is busy with laundry.

All sound effects are amplified, sharper throughout the rest of the play from now onwards.

LI NA　　　　The Gods are angry. The father of Thunder and the mother of Lightning. A warning.

KEVIN　　　　Superstitious are you?

LI NA　　　　Perhaps it's a sign.

KEVIN　　　　Did that help?

KEVIN　　　　Yea, I think so… he rubs the back of his head. Thanks.

LI NA　　　　I don't think you'll be leaving here anytime soon.

KEVIN　　　　Why not? *(gets up to look out of the window)* It's only thunder.

The sound of heavy rain follows.

LI NA   Ah ha. The Gods want you to stay after all.

KEVIN   The Gods do? It's got so dark out there, what time do you think it is now?

LI NA   Six-thirty.

KEVIN   Ah, traffic will be a nightmare at this time.

LI NA   You should check for weather updates.

KEVIN   I would but my phone is on the blink.

LI NA   We can use the radio.

Li Na turns the tuner, trying to get a signal. Muffled white noise sound. Kevin stands over her.

KEVIN   Wait, go back a bit.

Li Na turns the dial, nothing but white noise is heard.

LI NA   Nothing! I need to move it the other way.

KEVIN   There it is, I heard it.

Li Na turns the dial back, more white noise. Kevin moves over to the radio.

KEVIN   Let me. *(She gives him a look)* Sorry. Can I just have a go please?

Kevin turns the radio dial slowly, stopping every so often, ear to the speaker. Suddenly a new voice fills the room. It's a news report, muffled at first. He turns the dial with tiny movements.

RADIO ANNOUNCER   Concerns are growing in the search for the missing girl. She was last seen... *(He moves the tuner)* ... judge stands by his decision that it was the best for the future of the young man and that this was a one-off incident... *(Moves tuner, a weather report is heard, clearly audible)*

WEATHER PRESENTER In the southeast, the downpour is expected to continue through into late this evening. Main roads are currently closing and a red warning is issued for flooding. Roads that are closed off are High Burn Road, Chantley Drive, Parley Burn Road at the high street crossing. For more information, check online at BBC weather in your area...

Suddenly, the signal is lost.

KEVIN Was that Parley Burn Road?

LI NA Is that what you heard?

Kevin takes his phone from his pocket.

KEVIN Ah shit, nothing! *(He holds his phone up in the air, close to the window, moves around the room to get a signal)* Fuck!

LI NA Well, you're safe in here. There's nothing you can do.

Kevin tries the radio again, a few muffled voices but nothing audible.

LI NA You'll be here a while. Can I offer you something else to eat?

KEVIN I'll take that beer. *(She goes to the fridge, takes out a bottle of beer. It looks old.)* How long has that been in there?

LI NA A while. Do you think it will be okay to drink?

KEVIN Yea, yea, it'll be fine.

Li Na brings out wooden pieces, begins to join them together to build what looks like a clothes horse. She lays pieces of it around the room, forcing Kevin to move. She struggles to connect the pieces.

KEVIN   Here, let me help.

Kevin awkwardly stands over Li Na. They are very close, there is a tension. Kevin is distracted by the painting of the White Serpent in his eyeline.

LI NA   Do you like it? (*She watches him intensely.*)

KEVIN   It's... interesting

LI NA   It's mesmerising! It's one of my favourite paintings. Don't you think it's remarkable?

Kevin takes a good look at the painting. The white serpent coils around its prey. Li Na moves closer to Kevin, behind him, as he takes in the painting.

LI NA   Slow, delicate movements, soft, tender. Her beauty radiating in her human form. Bai Suzhen and Xu Xian, were lovers from other worlds. Forbidden by the laws of nature...

Li Na brushes past him to make her way back to the bucket of clothes. Kevin is a little uneasy with this move.

LI NA   Such a tragic tale.

Li Na wrings out items of clothing, jumpers, dresses, pillowcases etc and hangs them on the line.

Kevin moves back, not really sure what to do. The sound of rain falling heavily outside. He is distracted by the laundry which is dripping on the floor.

KEVIN   So a snake and a human?

LI NA   Yes.

KEVIN That's ridiculous!

LI NA It's symbolic. It resonates with all tragic love stories. They were kept apart, forced to stay away from one another. Animals have great importance in mythology, they were seen as equals or as superior to humans.

KEVIN I like that. I like animals. Do you have a basin to catch that water?

LI NA Of course you do, it's in your blood. *(She points to the second cupboard to the left.)*

KEVIN My blood? *(He investigates and finds a basin.)*

LI NA What I mean is, you have Suzi. You don't keep pets if you don't like animals. Especially cats. They can be trouble.

KEVIN Does Zhen Zhen ever come downstairs? Suzi would never be confined to one room.

LI NA *(taken aback)* Confined? No, Zhen Zhen can move freely. She chooses to stay up there. She is poorly. She prefers to stay in the bedroom.

KEVIN Is that why you stay indoors? Because of your sick cat?

LI NA Now you're being ridiculous.

Kevin is not convinced. Li Na moves towards the bookshelf.

LI NA There is a book I want you to have, it's somewhere in this pile. I have lots of folklore. Great myths I think you'd like...

KEVIN Does anyone visit you Li Na?

LI NA Sorry?

KEVIN Friends or family? You know, someone that pops round?

Li Na rummages through books on the shelf, piles of books and paper whose pages are wet now with the water on the floor. The wet pages spreading sodden with the laundry. Li Na steps carelessly on the pages and the clothes.

LI NA Now where has it gone? *(She finds a page, wet, dripping)* Ah, here it is, I think you'll like this one... *(Beat)* Once there was a shy and timid boy...

KEVIN Li Na, no more stories, yea?
(He moves over to the machine, away from the mess. Li Na is a little disappointed not to read the story, she tries to dry the page with her sleeve.) Look, while I'm here I'll see if I can wedge something in the machine to tighten the bearings, get the spin cycle to work for now. That would save you all of this mess.

LI NA You can do that?

KEVIN I think the spin would work.

LI NA Oh that would be wonderful!

Kevin goes to the machine and starts to put the parts back together.

7. TREE

LI NA And this tree
When it wants to, it opens up to you and lets you in.
You can climb inside its belly, sheltered from the cold

and harsh weather.
It will protect you.
It will save you from the people who hurt you, who chase you and beat you.
It offers you shelter and warmth.
It keeps you safe.

8. HOUSE

Kevin is working at the machine, Li Na is at the window, drying wet pages, hanging them around the room.
They sit in silence, with the sound of rain falling heavily outside.

KEVIN Can I ask you something? It's been playing on my mind since I got here?

LI NA Go on...

KEVIN How did you get my details?

LI NA Huh?

KEVIN You have no phone, no internet and you barely leave this house. So how did you get my number?

LI NA The stars aligned. You were brought to me. It is your destiny to be here at this very moment.

KEVIN I'm being serious.

LI NA So am I. This job you have – most of the time it is not so difficult for you. The hardest part is getting the work. But you come here and you're challenged.

Forced you to use your skills, and hone your craft. I pay you more than the standard fee. I'm keeping you in work. And now I shelter you from the storm.

KEVIN Yea, I'm grateful for the work but–

LI NA Maybe you were sent here. The universe brought you to this place for a reason. *(Kevin looks annoyed, folds his arms)* There is not a tiny little bit of you that believes in fate or karma?

KEVIN No. Why would I? Did you go looking for me?

Pause.

LI NA Yes, I did.

KEVIN Why? What do you want?

LI NA Do you have something to hide, Kevin?

KEVIN Who are you?

LI NA I am your worst nightmare!

KEVIN Who told you about me? Who are you?

LI NA *(laughs)* Your face, Kevin! I'm teasing you. I got it from Tesco. The Tesco delivery boy!

KEVIN Who?

LI NA He comes every Friday. You advertised in Tesco? The big store on the High Street? Your card was on the classified wall.

KEVIN ...

LI NA So the Tesco boy brought it to me when I complained about my machine.

Li Na goes to a kitchen drawer, fumbles around and produces the card and hands it to him.

KEVIN *(sheepishly)* I forgot I had put a card up there.

LI NA Are you alright?

KEVIN Yea…

LI NA Are you in some kind of trouble?

KEVIN No. No, I just get a bit spooked out in this forest, that's all.

LI NA Did something happen here?

A noise from upstairs, creaking sounds, not thuds, a hissing, snake like, quiet sound, just barely audible.

LI NA Something happened here.

KEVIN What is that?

Li Na sits on the chair, she takes a cigarette from her pocket, lights it, smoke swirls into the room, coils around them, snake-like.

LI NA In these woods a long, long time ago.

KEVIN What is that noise?

LI NA Once there was an old house, and the wind got into every crack and shook its bones, they shook so violently that the house woke up. The house remembered…

KEVIN What the…?

LI NA Drives Zhen Zhen mad…

KEVIN That's not a fucking cat! *(He moves towards the noise.)*

LI NA …running around the room, knocking things over, hiding keys…

KEVIN What is up there?

LI NA Climbing trees, skipping school, telling stories...

Li Na's skin changes, the scars beome more noticeable, each time the lightning strikes we see her scars more prominently, root-like; the shadows make them move, spreading over her body.

KEVIN What is happening to you?

LI NA ...this happened, or maybe it did not happen. The time has long past and much is forgotten, replaced, changed...

KEVIN Your hands,

LI NA Off kilter, losing balance...

KEVIN Your neck....

LI NA I don't think you are ready to see...

KEVIN See what?

LI NA Are you ready to see?

The sounds of thunder crashes, more heavy rain. Kevin is startled. The radio clicks on, white noise and audible voices can be heard coming from it.

RADIO ANNOUNCER ... A cold and harsh winter... *(The sound of white noise.)* ...What is she doing out here?... She's all alone...

KEVIN *(close to the radio)* the voice sounds familiar... What the...?

The voices come and go, as if the signal is dropping out, interspersed with the sound of white noise. He turns the tuner, trying to get the station back.

WEATHER PRESENTER We can expect more of a heavy downfall, avoid travel if you can... *(The sound of white noise.)* Missing now for two days, police are searching the areas, keep children indoors while the investigation continues... *(The sound of white noise.)*

Kevin lifts the radio and turns the dial. A hissing sound is heard, snake-like, growing louder, hissing his name, the picture of the white serpent lights up, smoke enveloping the room.

RADIO ANNOUNCER *(whispers)* Kai Wen. Kai Wen. Don't move...

Kevin drops the radio in fright, trips over a pot. It makes a clatter and water spills.

KEVIN   Shit!

He looks around for something to mop up the mess, in the machine, he sees something still inside, he pulls it out, a white thread, thick. As he pulls it becomes red, thick blood clots drip from it, he pulls this thread/flesh-like material, it's attached to a white t-shirt, a child's, with blood stains.

KEVIN   Don't move.
I can't stay here.
I have to get away.
Mum asking me.
Don't move, she says.
Tell me, she says.
But I can't say the words.
They're in my mouth but I can't get them out.
They're stuck.
Don't move.
Whose blood is it, Kai Wen?
She says.
Whose blood is it, Kai Wen?

That's not my name.
That's not who I am, anymore.
We moved.
We got away.
That's not me.
That's not who I am.
Not anymore

Li Na's smoke swirls, fills the space, the hissing grows louder, a snake presence in the room. Kevin chokes, struggles to breathe.

9. TREE

LI NA Shall we begin? *(He nods)*
There is a tree. A momentous tree.

KEVIN A monstrous tree

LI NA Towering over us

KEVIN We're playing

LI NA A magnificent tree

KEVIN We're climbing, building dens

LI NA A magnanimous tree

KEVIN Nothing else to do around here

LI NA A mnemonic tree?

KEVIN We should have been in school

LI NA A magical tree

KEVIN It's getting late

LI NA Sun splitting the trees with the threat of leaving for good.

KEVIN	A figure in the distance
LI NA	Small
KEVIN	Look
LI NA	A girl
KEVIN	Her there
LI NA	Lost
KEVIN	What's she doing out here?
LI NA	Alone
KEVIN	Wait
LI NA	She stands on small legs
KEVIN	We know her from school, she's younger than us, her sister's in our year.
LI NA	Small legs that will splay out
KEVIN	It's getting dark. I can tell with the shadows on the trees.
LI NA	Little arms
KEVIN	Do it, they said, she'll do
LI NA	Reaching
KEVIN	I don't want to but my mates are making me do this – they're mocking me
LI NA	Stretching
KEVIN	I can't be twelve and never have kissed a girl
LI NA	Connecting
KEVIN	And this tree, when it wants to, it lets you in.

LI NA	Touching
KEVIN	We can climb inside. Away from the people who hurt us, who chase us and beat us.
LI NA	I don't want to do this
KEVIN	They're going to know if I don't
LI NA	I want to go home
KEVIN	Just, wait
LI NA	I want my sister
KEVIN	She left you out here in the woods
LI NA	I have to find her
KEVIN	You can't go back out there
LI NA	No
KEVIN	Come on, just let me…
LI NA	No…
KEVIN	Don't leave. Please I grab her arm, I pull her back I shake her Just a little I didn't mean for her… She's so light, Feather-like She loses her balance Falls Head on rock Blood on stone Mates come looking She's out cold But still breathing

Skirt hitched up at her waist
Knickers exposed
Curiosity on their faces
They want to touch her
No, wait
Don't do that
Their hands are on her
I can't watch them...
I can't move
I can't.
No words
But no words come out

Pause.

LI NA There is a tree
A momentous tree
Born from girl
The start of a cold harsh winter
Seeped into her lungs
A little girl who stayed too long inside the tree
The opening closed and she was stuck inside for eternity.
Her arms stretched, sinew and flesh turning into branches reaching, extending up to the sky.
Her legs splayed, transforming into roots, moving down burying deep under the ground beneath the world
She becomes part of the tree
Her heart in its centre.

KEVIN The rain fell
The boys ran
I tried to get her up
Blood on my t-shirt
She wouldn't move
I panicked.

I didn't know what to do
So like the boys, I ran.
I kept running until I got home.
How was I to know the weather would change?
How was I to know it would get so cold?
How was I to know she didn't wake up, her sister
couldn't find her, her family searched all night for her,
The missing person in the news was her,
The reason we moved away is her,
I would wake up in the middle of the night and see her,
Lying there,
Their faces,
Their hands,
Her voice in my sleep.
I thought she was okay
I thought she was okay.
They sent me away, my name changed to something similar, not too different.
So he'll forget after time, he'll not remember this, and over time his memory will fade.
(Pause.)
This happened. Or maybe in my mind it did not happen. The time has long past and much is forgotten, replaced, changed, fabricated, stories with new layers and layers...
I couldn't... I didn't mean to...
I didn't do anything to her.
I didn't touch her.

LI NA   You didn't stop them.
You were witness to it.
You could have stopped it.
You could have changed the story.
Why did you come here? Kai Wen?
Why did you come here?

10. HOUSE

The walls have more cracks than before. The walls of the set collapse to reveal the inside of a tree with large roots. The washing machine lights up, vibrates to give a beating heart sound. Kevin falls to his knees.

KEVIN I came here to remember,
I remember
I remember
I remember
I remember

Lights fade.

The End.

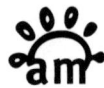

Aurora Metro Books

BRITISH EAST ASIAN PLAYS eds. Cheryl Robson, Amanda Rogers and Ashley Thorpe, seven plays by writers of Chinese descent
ISBN 978-1- 912430-08-6 £16.99

SOUTHEAST ASIAN PLAYS ed. Cheryl Robson and Aubrey Mellor
ISBN 978-1-906582-86-9   £16.99

THE DUTIFUL DAUGHTER by Charles Way (English-Mandarin edition)
ISBN 978-0-9546912-6-4 £7.99

COMBUSTION by Asif Khan
ISBN 978-1-911501-91-6   £9.99

THE DIARY OF A HOUNSLOW GIRL by Ambreen Razia
ISBN 978-0-9536757-9-1   £8.99

SPLIT/MIXED by Ery Nzaramba
ISBN 978-1-911501-97-8   £10.99

THE TROUBLE WITH ASIAN MEN by Sudha Bhuchar, Kristine Landon-Smith and Louise Wallinger
ISBN 978-1-906582-41-8   £8.99

SIX PLAYS BY BLACK AND ASIAN WOMEN WRITERS ed. Kadija George
ISBN 978-0-9515877-2-0   £12.99

BLACK AND ASIAN PLAYS Anthology introduced by Afia Nkrumah
ISBN 978-0-9536757-4-6   £12.99

NEW SOUTH AFRICAN PLAYS ed. Charles J. Fourie
ISBN 978-0-9542330-1-3   £11.99

DURBAN DIALOGUES, INDIAN VOICE by Ashwin Singh
ISBN 978-1-906582-42-5   £15.99

WOMEN OF ASIA by Asa Palomera
ISBN 978-1-906582-94-4   £7.99

HARVEST by Manjula Padmanabhan
ISBN 978-0-9536757-7-7   £6.99

I HAVE BEFORE ME A REMARKABLE DOCUMENT by Sonja Linden
ISBN 978-0-9546912-3-3   £7.99

www.aurorametro.com